With great love and  shares the true story of his p Christ. In these pages, reader journey from fear, isolation, and confusion to a life of restored masculinity and authentic freedom. This daring personal testimony will change lives by drawing hearts to the healing love of God.

Lisa Mladinich
Breakthrough Coach, Best-selling Author

I know David well…and I know his story. And yet, this heartfelt and vulnerable account was riveting. David offers a rare glimpse into the inner world of someone whose attractions were shaped in a crucible of pain and anchored into his psyche by the lies of bullies and the bullying lies he came to accept. His journey toward healing is a triumph of God's merciful love and truth- a light in this dark world offering real hope to the many who struggle to find their true identities in Christ. One word- Inspiring.

Allison Ricciardi, LMHC
Founder and President: Catholictherapists.com
Director: TheRaphaelRemedy.com

David Prosen's My Journey to Truth, Authentic Love and Hope is a candid, moving, and insightful narrative of God's grace working wonderfully in David's life. The book will be especially helpful for anyone who struggles with a troubled childhood or with sexual temptation. David's story will inspire and provide hope. He is a model of courage for all of us.

Dr. Patrick Lee
McAleer Professor of Bioethics
Director of the Center for Bioethics at
Franciscan University of Steubenville

My Journey to Truth, Authentic Love and Hope

*One Man's Story of Transformation
and Chastity Through Christ*

My Journey to Truth, Authentic Love and Hope

*One Man's Story of Transformation
and Chastity Through Christ*

Copyright © 2019 by David Prosen.

Contents

Dedications   7

Foreword   9

My Journey to Truth, Authentic Love
and Hope   12

A Message to Those Who Experience
Same-sex Attractions   47

Acknowledgements   48

Notes   50

Dedications

To my brothers and sisters in Christ who experience same-sex attractions and who are striving to live chaste lives as well as their family members who love them dearly. The world tells us that something is wrong with pursuing chastity because it is impossible to obtain. The world tells us the Church is cruel for asking us to pursue living a chaste life. Chastity is not only possible, but life fulfilling, meaningful, beautiful and peaceful. Getting there cannot be done on our own merit. We must seek God and have brothers and sisters who can walk with us on this journey. Please check out Courage and EnCourage International if you haven't already. This beautiful ministry can provide you with support and resources. May God bless you on this journey with true friendship and more importantly bless you with His truth, authentic love and hope.

To all priest, bishops and shepherds of this beautiful Church. May God bless you with the Graces you need to shepherd us in His truth, authentic love and hope. Your job is not an easy one. I want to thank the many who have touched my life and were Christ to me. May God continue to give you the Graces to be Christ to all of us.

Foreword

There is so much misinformation and ideological falsehood promoted in American culture these days concerning anything related to sexuality and gender. In the midst of all the confusion, David Prosen is a calm voice of truth who speaks with sincerity and conviction. No one can tell David the "real truth" about gender identity and the LGBT lifestyle, because he already knows it from the inside. He knows the emptiness of trying to live a life in denial of our masculinity or femininity, which God gives to each one of us as a gift. He also knows the emptiness of trying to cure emotional wounds through sexual experiences and short-term relationships. He has found peace in God, but knows better than to promise others that this peace is magical and instantaneous, if you just "pray the right prayer" and are "truly sincere." As David knows, finding peace in God is a journey that begins with taking up one's cross daily and following Jesus, and continues in that way to the end of our lives.

I wish every adult Catholic in America would read David's testimony, whether they experience same- or opposite-sex attractions. For those who experience same-sex attraction, they will find in David a friend who has shared many of their same experiences and pain, yet found a path forward to embrace God's plan for our sexuality and in this way experience love, self-respect, and peace. For those who do not experience same-sex attractions, David's story will help them understand their friends who do. But more than that, David has things to teach all of us about how to heal from the emotional wounds of our childhoods and upbringing; how to forgive those who hurt, manipulated, or abused us; how to attain a healthy sense of our self-identity as sons and daughters of God.

I was deeply moved, and still am, by David's testimony, which is often raw in its transparency. Like many, many other men, I could relate on a deep level with his insecurities about fitting in with the "world of men" and his struggle to find acceptance and approval from the various men in his life, especially his father. Many men who never have same-sex attraction also have these experiences of insecurity and rejection, and learn to cope in different ways, not all of which are healthy or holy. Reading David's testimony made me more aware of the way my own sense of myself as a man has been shaped by the sometimes painful or traumatic events of my childhood and adolescence, and his courage in facing reality, the Truth, and his fears head on has inspired me to make progress in my own journey to be a healthier and holier Catholic man. I repeat: David has a lot to teach all of us, both men and women, who are seeking God and trying to come to grips with the mystery of our masculinity or femininity. I heartily recommend this book.

Dr. John Bergsma
Catholic Bible Scholar
Author and Speaker
February 2019

My Journey to Truth, Authentic Love and Hope

*One Man's Story of Transformation
and Chastity Through Christ*

Masculinity:
Something to Be Feared

I was born in the winter of 1962 to a young couple. I have a very vivid memory, from when I was only two years old of being awakened by a loud booming sound. I stood up in my crib and felt terrified. After this, I heard my father screaming and yelling while my mother was crying. What was going on? My peaceful sleep had been interrupted, and I felt so afraid. I cried while standing in my crib trying to see what was happening. My father came into the room and picked me up. I think he tried to calm me down, but it just wasn't working. He brought me into my parent's bedroom, and as we walked past the door, I noticed a giant gaping hole in the upper center of it.

I saw my mom sitting up in her bed sobbing. I didn't understand what was happening, but I did know that I didn't feel safe in my father's arms. Why was there a hole in the door? Why was my mommy crying? I pointed to Mom, screaming as loud as I could as tears poured down my face. I was hoping they would understand what I was trying to communicate. In between her tears, I heard Mom say, "Take him out of here." I felt scared, threatened and now rejected. I remember screaming and crying and my dad saying,

"He doesn't want me. He wants you." Those words were not only true at that moment, but also prophetic in a sense. This was the beginning seed of fear towards my dad, which would continue to grow and play out much in my life.

Later, as an adult, my mom filled in the gaps of my memory of that day. I was told that my dad had been angry, and my mom had locked the door out of fear. He became filled with rage, screaming, "You will never lock me out of any door," and had slammed his fist into the door, creating the large hole. I learned that she told him to take me out of the room because she believed she needed to be strong and was embarrassed for her little boy to see her cry.

A year after this incident, my younger sister Darlene joined our little family. Like many siblings, Darlene and I didn't get along as children; we fought constantly. But this eventually changed, and we became close friends by the time we reached our teens.

My mother and I were very close, and my father and I were not. As shown in the above example, he could be filled with anger or rage. He often physically and emotionally abused me. I have numerous memories of being thrown in the corner and being punched or beaten with a belt by my red-faced father, screaming obscenities with spit spraying from his mouth.

There were also many times in which Darlene and I would get into an argument or fight. Darlene learned how to get even with me when she was mad. She learned that if she started a fight with me, I would get beaten by Dad. It didn't matter who started it; it was my fault. She was his little girl and could do no wrong.

Dad was very talented in landscaping, woodworking and fixing up old cars. The problem was that he had so much anger inside him that as he went about his work, he would slam things and swear. As I grew older, he tried to pass his knowledge on to me, but almost every time, it ended up in him losing his patience, screaming curse words, and calling me names.

My father wasn't into sports at all, and as a result, I didn't learn the basic concepts or skills needed to play baseball, football, or basketball. At school, I quickly learned that I wasn't like most of the other boys. I was one of the last picked for teams and my peers who ended up with me, loudly complained and made it clear that I wasn't wanted. I tried to learn, but no one took the time to teach me and encourage me. And with each attempt, my peers would laugh and tell me that I threw like a girl. The message I got was,

"You don't belong; you're not like us; you're not one of us boys."

Now, many boys, in situations like this, might think, "I'll prove you wrong," and then give it their all to show they could do it. From a place of confidence, they take the risk. If they fail, they pick themselves up and try again and persevere until they achieve their goal. Usually they have someone who has given them some confidence or encouragement to take risks; someone who believes in them and cheers them on. If the coach or peers told them they couldn't do it, I watched as these boys proved them wrong by completing the task, whether it was throwing, hitting, or catching a ball, etc. But I lacked the guidance and encouragement, and my confidence was extremely low because of what was happening at home. I believed that I didn't have what it took and that there was no hope for me to succeed in this area because I was different from the other boys.

There were some gym activities, like wrestling and dodgeball, that I dreaded because it was opportunities for the bullies to cause pain, fear, and humiliation. I would hear, "Prosen, I am going to kick your a--." I hated gym class. Intense shame and self-loathing kept me from taking the risk, and instead of proving them wrong, I believed they were right.

In addition to this, I was bullied by some neighborhood kids, and as I grew older, the tormenting increased at school. I was teased for being chubby and for not being like them. Soon, the names evolved into, "girl," "sissy" and "wuss" and, starting in junior high, "queer," "fag" and "faggot."

I desperately longed to be like the boys, but because of experiences with my father, peers, and bullies, masculinity terrified me. For the most part, the good qualities of manhood were not shown to me. I didn't feel protected or encouraged nor was I given guidance to succeed, which are the kinds of things a good father would do for his son. There were some times my dad and male acquaintances reached out to me in positive ways, but the negative aspects of masculinity shown to me far outweighed these few positive ones. The intense inner shame kept me from accepting and embracing these fleeting moments of encouragement.

Different;
Not Like the Others

As long as I can remember, I have experienced attractions towards the same sex. This began before I knew anything about sexuality. Later in life, I used to think this was proof that I was born gay. But it wasn't proof, and for me, there were reasons for these attractions. Most children have heroes or those they look up to. Mine weren't necessarily superheroes (although I did love Batman), but rather my male peers, those who had physical or emotional traits that I did not possess.

Admiration of others is healthy, but in my case, this admiration became distorted out of my deep shame and inner turmoil. In regards to my peers who I looked up to, I used to think, "If only I looked like him or I was strong like him or athletic like him, then maybe I would fit in and not feel so alone." In a sense, I was coveting these traits, thinking I was flawed and not likable, while these other boys who I put on a pedestal, were popular, handsome, strong and confident.

I began to hate who I was and desperately wished I could be like one of them. Then the unthinkable happened – puberty. The attraction or admiration or coveting (whatever you want to call it) had now taken a turn and had become sexualized. There were a couple of boys who I experimented with. I believe it was more about exploring our bodies. However, I did experience sexual sensations, and this only confused me more. I soon learned about masturbation. This along with my fantasies and continued coveting of masculine traits that I perceived I lacked, further sexualized these attractions – that weren't sexual in the first place.

As mentioned, I had always felt different. But now, with the attraction being sexualized, this feeling of being different worsened and sank to an even lower level. I felt like a freak and hated who I was. As I entered high school, the loneliness was immobilizing. I befriended some females who were older than me, but the loneliness remained. I felt so different, and the self-loathing continued to grow. Daily, I was bullied and called "fag" and "faggot." In one class, when the teacher turned to write on the board, a bully sitting behind me would often flick the back of my head, quietly saying, "Prosen, you're a faggot."

I hated gym class and was elated to learn that we only had to take gym as freshmen in high school. This would be my last time of dealing with the taunts. However, I found out that a requirement was that we had to change into shorts to participate. I was in the middle of puberty and was ashamed, not only of the changes in my body (that no one spoke to me about) but of the sexual sensations as well, that often occurred when I saw attractive male peers. I was terrified of the locker room and everything it represented to me. After all, only the guys were allowed in there, and I certainly didn't feel like one of them.

I worried that maybe they were right, and I was gay. I was petrified that if I changed in the locker room or showered with them, they would have somehow figured out that I was sexually attracted to some of them. And if this happened, I knew that this would exacerbate the already occurring torment and bullying. As a result, I chose not to participate in gym class that year and sat on the bench during the entire period. Unfortunately, this horrible decision led to the consequence of my failing gym and having to "take it over again" or "repeat it," but this time with those younger than me. Once again, I was made fun of as these younger peers laughed and wondered what was wrong with me, that I had failed gym. This time, I forced myself to change into shorts, because I was not going to do this again. Although I did put on shorts to participate, I refused to go anywhere near that shower, and I didn't care how bad I smelled as a result.

When I was about fifteen or sixteen, a twenty-one-year-old befriended me. I looked up to this guy as an older brother, and it was terrific to have another male look at me as a male and not as a freak. After about one week of hanging out, I stayed the night at his house, and he made a pass at me. He played head games with me, and I was confused and miserable. I was too young to understand what I had gotten myself into let alone to recognize the manipulation and control that was occurring. Also, the ever-growing shame deep inside my heart was now overflowing.

I remember thinking that it was now official: my peers were right in calling me a fag or faggot. I called the 700 Club TV show help line and spoke to a woman named Mrs. Brown. She told me that homosexuality was a sin. I had never heard this or anything about homosexuality ever mentioned in my church. I gave my life to Christ and broke up with this guy several days later. At first, I was on an emotional high, but I didn't understand my faith, nor the sacraments, especially the Real Presence of Jesus Christ in the Holy Eucharist. Eventually, the emotional high dissipated and I went back to thinking I was gay and all alone as I continued to live in isolation at school.

Acceptance of the Gay Identity

I longed for my eighteenth birthday because this would be the day when I would go to my first gay bar and meet others like myself. Sure enough, on the very day I turned eighteen I did. At first, it was exciting and so much fun to be with others that I could relate to. And maybe just maybe, I would find a good-looking guy who would love me for me. I never found him, although I saw many men and experienced much heartache and loneliness. I was even traumatically raped in one of my first relationships at eighteen years of age. After a couple of years of living actively in the gay culture, out of curiosity, I wrote out all those who I had been sexually intimate with. At the time, it totaled almost a hundred, and I wasn't even trying to be promiscuous, at least not yet.

I was trying to find a man to love me. There were several times that I would turn to God out of my pain. Usually, I would experience an emotional high from attending a retreat or surrendering to God. But these highs didn't last long, and when the high disappeared, I went back to living an active gay life searching for a man who could rescue me by loving me. Each time I did this, I found myself falling even deeper into sin, to dull the pain and overwhelming loneliness. I recently found a poem I wrote while I was living the gay life. I think it shows the immense pain I experienced during this time:

Untitled Poem

Loneliness engulfs me in its river.
It carries me to the lake of darkness.
I can't find a stable rock to hold on
to as the turbulent water flows.
At times, I thought I had grabbed
onto one that was set solidly in the soil.
One so strong that it can hold me
and be my home.
One that I can trust and depend on.
But each time, after giving it my all
and putting effort, time and trust in
building the home.
The rock slips from the stable ground
and once again carries me with it in
the turbulent waters.
Once again, I am lost, and caught
in the pains of loneliness.

I thought it couldn't get worse, but then my sister, Darlene, who I was very close to, died suddenly and unexpectedly at the age of twenty-one. I remember thinking that all the pain I had experienced in my life was nothing compared to losing her. Once I worked through some of my grief, I couldn't help but face my own mortality. I also felt much guilt. "It should have been me, not her." I was the one slowly killing himself with drugs, sex (especially in the middle the AIDS crisis) and driving drunk and/or high.

A Little Hope and a Lot of Shame

I obtained a transfer and promotion from my job and moved to Florida for a year where my grandma lived. I decided there had to be something more to God than an emotional high. I knew from the Parable of the Seed that I needed to have a strong foundation to build my relationship with God on. I became active in the Church and sought out God in a personal way, as I slowly started to learn some things about my faith. After moving back to Ohio, I continued to seek out and understand who God was. The intense pain of grief in my heart slowly began to heal. I felt God's comfort as I continued in my journey of healing. This was important because Darlene's death was the motivating event that caused me to turn to Christ. I found a poem I wrote during this period, which reflects the healing power of my Heavenly Father during this pivotal time:

Reflections

Reflections of his blue eyes bounce
off the pane of glass.
Cold and sad blue eyes slowly fade
as several large trees adjust to focus.
Mounds of rich green leaves
protrude out of each branch.
Memories begin to focus and center
from his mind and heart.
A little boy and his sister swinging
from a tire suspended from one of those trees.
Reflections of his sad blue eyes appear
again through the pane of glass.
He's reminded that these memories are
days of the past and can never return.
Reflections of his sad blue eyes fade
again as he is overwhelmed by the
massive gray sky.
It seems to envelop the earth with its
gloom and despair reminding him
of the reality of his loss.
His sister, friend and a genuine part
of him is gone and never to return.
Reflections of his sad blue eyes
now fill with tears from the aching
pain of sorrow and loneliness.
He looks up and begs God to ease

the pain.
He closes his eyes and still sees the
reflection of those sad blue eyes in his mind.
Very slowly, with eyes still closed,
a new scene bounces off the pane of glass
and adjusts into focus.
He sees two figures one on each side
of him. Jesus on one side wiping his
tears and his sister on the other.
He feels an intense compassion nothing
like he had felt before as he sees
and feels Christ's hand on his shoulder.
His sister pleaded with God to do
something to ease her brother's pain.
He looked at her with deep love and
said, "My child, it is already done."
Reflections of his blue eyes bounce off
the pane of glass as he opens his eyes.
This time the sadness is replaced with hope.

Now those of you who may have seen a small version of my testimony in the film, *The Third Way: Homosexuality and the Catholic Church*, may notice something different in what I am about to say.[1] The following was edited out for the sake of time, but I believe it is a vital piece of my testimony. In addition to the healing of grief, for five and a half years I abstained from sexual acting out as well as stopped alcohol and drug abuse. Even more profound was that I verbally forgave my father.

However, despite these very positive things that were happening in my life, I was living an emotional hell every day. Sexual attraction, whether it is to the opposite sex or the same sex has a biological component to it. Whenever I noticed or interacted with a guy who I found good-looking, I experienced physiological sensations like butterflies in my stomach, sweaty palms and accelerated heart rate, excitement; sometimes I even stuttered. This happened many times, every single day of those five and a half years. I begged God for a cure – to take this from me. These biological reactions in my body caused me to feel shame. I thought I was sinning and I felt evil and horrible. (Just to be clear, the Church teaches these biological reactions are not sinful. I am so grateful to the priest who helped me to understand the truth about this when I brought it up in the confessional.)

Back to the Gay Life

The sexual attractions remained. Some friends told me that maybe I was sinning in some other area of my life or perhaps I wasn't praying hard enough. These statements only increased my shame. Then a friend of mine suggested that maybe God wasn't curing me because maybe there wasn't anything wrong with being gay. I thought about this. Given how sincere I had been in begging God for assistance, I couldn't help but think my friend had a valid point. I chose to go back into the gay life and this time do it "the right way," so-to-speak, by not getting drunk or having promiscuous sex and maybe even finding a Christian man. Well, I couldn't find the "right" way to live in the gay life and found myself slipping into old habits. An exception was that at one point I ended up in a relationship with a man that lasted one year to the day. Before this, I not had a relationship last more than three months.

God uses all things for the good for those who love him. Through this experience of a more committed relationship, God taught me some essential truths about what love really is. It's not an emotional high like I thought, but instead, a commitment, hanging in there and working things through. Yes, love is a choice and can evolve into an emotion.

Later I learned that the emotional high or "magic" when I first met someone was infatuation. I believe this infatuation can be felt much stronger than love because it is based solely on emotions and natural feelings in the body. However, as authentic love blossoms, it is much more powerful and beautiful than infatuation because it is so much more than emotions and feelings. It's about choice, about sacrifice and hanging in there and working it through even if it hurts. Love grows and flourishes over time and in my opinion, doesn't happen at first sight.

After the break-up, I realized that maybe one of the problems was that this guy wasn't a Christian. At this point, I had already stopped going to Church and was thinking I needed to work on my relationship with Christ again.

Hope Springs from Truth

A friend of mine who is a deacon invited me to come back to the Catholic Church. When I told him I couldn't go, because I was gay, he suggested I still go but also pray and sincerely ask God to show me the truth. I didn't go to the Catholic Church as he asked, but I did begin to pray and ask God to show me His truth. My deacon friend was right. If we ask God to show us the truth and we are sincere in wanting this, God will show it to us, but in His time.

I went on a quest and visited all the LGBT

churches in my area. I eventually stopped having sex and decided that I would not have a relationship until I met a Christian gay man who I was attracted to and with whom I shared similar values and beliefs. I never found him.

However, as you can see, my heart started slowly opening back up to Christ. As this happened, I began to yearn for Him and His truth. One day, I felt Him say to my heart, "Yes David, you never chose this attraction, but you can choose whether you act on this attraction."

As simple as this sounds, I was relieved to discover that I could choose between continuing to act on this physical/emotional attraction and live chastely. Before this, I thought my only choices were either continuing to live as I was as a gay man or going back to living in shame.

So far, I had been miserable with every approach I had tried living with same-sex attractions. I had been miserable when I felt different in school; I had been miserable when I identified and lived as a gay man; I had been miserable when I asked God to cure me and He didn't; and I had been miserable when I tried to find a Christian man who would love me for me and couldn't find one.

Finally, I opened the Catechism of the Catholic

Church for maybe the first time and read about homosexuality.[2] I felt so much freedom in learning that this was a trial or cross that I had to carry. We all have our crosses to bear.

"Then Jesus told his disciples, 'If any man would come after me, let him deny himself and take up his cross and follow me.'" (Mt 16:24, Ignatius RSV)

I felt a sense of freedom because I knew that although He might not cure me, He certainly would give me the graces I needed to carry this cross. I began concentrating on living a celibate life. Even though it took a long time and there were many valleys through which I would have to travel, eventually, by God's grace, I began pursuing and living a chaste life (including no masturbation). The first time I stopped living the gay life, I begged God for a cure many times daily and felt much shame as a result. This time, I didn't ask for a cure and instead, prayed for the strength I needed to carry my crosses and grow in holiness. It was difficult and a long journey but this time there was peace instead of shame. My challenging path to becoming chaste is dealt with more in my book, *Accompanying Those with Same-sex*

Attractions: A Guide for Catholics.[3] I began discovering the beautiful treasures of our Catholic Faith which help us, particularly the sacraments of Reconciliation and of the Holy Eucharist and obtained much strength from them.

I still felt so incredibly alone and strongly desired to find others who were on this journey. Courage International is an apostolate which provides support groups for men and women who experience same-sex attractions who are striving to follow the teachings of the Church. There wasn't a Courage chapter in my area, and I longed for this kind of support. So I joined I an online email group and obtained that support I was looking for. It was so refreshing to know there were others like myself who were focused on growing closer to Christ and following or striving to follow the Church's teachings.

Eventually, praise God, I was able to stop masturbation and fully live a life of chastity. I am so grateful. I still have my issues, as we all do, but living a chaste life is so much more meaningful.

Healings of Old Wounds

After much prayer and discernment, I enrolled at the Franciscan University of Steubenville. I took one year of theology classes and then pursued and obtained a master's degree in counseling with a certificate of concentration in Christian counseling. But I am getting ahead of myself. I went for the degree and education, but Christ had something else in mind as well. This was the beginning of the healing that He began to do in my heart.

One of the first experiences of healing happened on a graduate nontraditional student retreat. For one of the talks, they separated the men and women. We listened to a presentation by two men who told us what it meant to be Catholic men of God. They were the stereotypical macho type of men that I used to be afraid of. They spoke gruffly in deep, loud voices and kept relating everything in football terms. As I sat there, I started feeling frustrated. By the end of the talk, I was furious. I smoked at the time and spent much of the rest of the retreat outside with my cigarettes. On my way home, I kept asking God, "Why?" And then I asked myself, "Why? Why did I go on this stupid retreat? I could have spent time working on my paper that was due, but no, I chose this instead."

When I got home, I journaled quite a bit. What came out of this was profound. I learned that I never let go of that anger towards those male peers of mine who taunted me when I was growing up. I projected my anger onto these two men and many other men throughout my life, who had very macho personas and often spoke of sports, cars or "broads." I forgave those childhood peers of mine, knowing that forgiveness is a process and not something that happens immediately. At the next mass I attended at the university, I was kneeling and praying to God, asking what He wanted me to do about those two men who spoke at the retreat. I heard some noise next to me, opened my eyes and looked to my left, and there kneeling next to me, was one of the two guys. I looked up and quietly said, "That is very funny, God." But then the words "sign of peace" came to my mind. And I realized at that moment that this was a wonderful gift from God. That sign of peace wasn't just a symbol of offering peace to my neighbor, but instead represented a reconciliation of past hurt and pain projected onto men like him.

The healings continued. I made some Catholic male friendships at Franciscan University and asked two of them who loved baseball to teach me how to throw, catch and hit, and they did. I never realized that there was a specific way to hold the ball. No wonder, I was made fun of for the way I threw. Slowly, I began to see real progress in that I could catch, hit and throw. As a result, I gained some confidence. I even played every Sunday in an informal co-ed softball game with the graduate and non-traditional students. Me! The one who was terrified of sports. There were emotionally painful and awkward moments at times when I had some flashbacks about team members who expressed anger when frustrated about a play. However, I chose to fight the old memories and embraced the reality of where I was at in that moment. I realized that this anger wasn't abusive like in my past but, rather was expressed very differently by mature Christians who were able to calm down quickly and let go of it. This helped model to me healthy ways of expressing anger helping me see that anger doesn't have to be something hurtful and feared. This, of course, brought more healing and my confidence continued to grow.

As I mentioned, when I had identified as gay and lived the gay life, I had many sexual experiences with men. In looking back, we used each other as objects. In addition to them, I had sexually acted out with two different female friends. I wasn't sexually attracted to them but was emotionally attracted to them, since they were good friends. This was somewhat confusing to me since the first time it happened, my female friend was the initiator, and I wasn't into it at all and only went along with it because I didn't want to hurt her. She realized from my response that I wasn't into this and apologized. We agreed to never do this again. However, about a year later, I started thinking about it and thought, "it wasn't that bad," and this time, I initiated it after a night of many drinks which ultimately led to a very unhealthy pattern; we would both go to the gay bars, get drunk and if we didn't meet anyone, we would sometimes mess around sexually. This hurt our friendship with confusion and unclear boundaries. I didn't learn from this mistake, because much later, this happened with another one of my female friends. It is never good to bring friendship to a sexual level. When this happens, there is the risk of the bond being tainted by the two using each other for pleasure or comfort, and it can bring confusion and hurt feelings.

I am sharing my experiences with the two different female friends because something unusual for me began to happen as God brought healings to old wounds in my life. As I mentioned, the attraction to the two female friends was more of an emotional one. However, with some of the healing I experienced beginning at Franciscan University, I began to appreciate a woman's physical beauty in a way that I hadn't before (not just emotionally, but physically as well.) I have not dated, and I'm not sure what God has planned, but I am open to doing His will, whatever that is.

Real Masculinity:
Something to be Embraced and Accepted

The healing has continued over the years. One of the most profound healings came about after working with a life coach about ten years ago. Earlier, I discussed my horrible experiences in the locker room while growing up. As an adult, I joined a gym, and the fear was still present. Those memories and painful emotions from high school were still there in my heart and in my mind.

I felt very different in high school. I never thought I was a woman trapped in a man's body, but the problem is, I never felt like a man either. I felt as though I did not belong to this mysterious world of men and masculinity. My life coach asked me to face my fears and participate in the locker room. This meant, showering, changing clothes and noticing all the men there. He didn't want me to look down and pretend like I didn't see anything, nor did he want me to gawk. Instead he just wanted me to be present and notice my environment and the men in it. He wanted me to nonchalantly observe all of the men: those that were good-looking, muscled and buff, those with average looks, those who were heavy and thin, older and younger. He wanted me to notice all of them and then ask myself, "Where do I fit in this world of men?"

As I walked in, I began to feel a sense of panic and imagined I would be yelled at and told that I needed to leave because I didn't belong. I knew that this wasn't logical and more than likely would not happen. But the panic and the emotions and thoughts were so intense that it was hard to accept logic.

To my surprise, I wasn't screamed at or told to leave. In fact, several men spoke to me. I was shocked, and this was life-changing for me. It was at this point in my life that I came to realize that I do, in fact, belong to the world of men. Praise God! This was tremendous healing for me since masculinity always terrified me. I began to learn that I possessed masculine traits all along. My life coach and I discussed my childhood. I started to see that although I didn't like sports, nor was I athletic or interested in cars, I did love a lot of things that appealed to males: climbing trees, adventures, exploring caves, stories and movies of pirates, monsters and danger. My life coach helped me to affirm that little boy inside me who after these years, still lives in my heart.

Am I cured? No. I don't like that word. But as

discussed, I have received several experiences of healing that continue to bring peace to my heart. Healing needs to be seen on a continuum. Some people who, after trying to follow the Lord, experience no redemption in their same-sex attractions, are frustrated and go back to embracing a LGBT identity. Our culture says this is how it is for everyone. But this just isn't true. Some, whose attractions persist, are actually able to find peace and freedom in living out their faith in a chaste life. This, by the way, can be considered healing, especially for those who were addicted to porn, masturbation, sex, and/or relationships. Still others truly experience a slight or even a dramatic decrease in their same-sex attractions. I know some people who are married to the opposite sex and living fulfilling lives after having once lived as a LGBT identified individual in the past. I know I could get married if that's what God wants for me. I'm not rushing anything. I am still working on me, and more importantly, God is still working on me.

Some have said to me, "David, I don't know anyone who has had the attraction go away completely, one hundred percent." I think I have an explanation for this. I believe all of us, as human beings, experience same-sex attractions. I don't mean sexual or eroticized ones, but attractions to the good.

We tend to gravitate towards those we are attracted to. Maybe I am attracted to my friend's strength, or his courage, or his sense of humor, or his patience, or his compassion, or his smile, or his talents, or maybe it's just how I see Jesus in that person's eyes. It's natural and good to be attracted to people and this includes people of the same-sex. As individuals, we typically don't want to be friends with those with traits that we view as "unattractive." All of our have friends have faults, because all of us humans have them. At the same time, I don't know many people who seek out friends who are known to be hateful, hostile, hurtful, selfish, gossipy, mean, users, murderers, liars, etc.

We are naturally attracted to the good, and we are made this way. Many people, including myself, look for friends who are loyal, trustworthy, and honest. For many of us, this is a criterion for who we want to be best friends with. I believe this natural attraction to the good that we all experience might be the reason why we don't know many people who have had an attraction to the same-sex disappear one hundred percent. Do I still experience same-sex attractions? Yes, and the vast majority of the time it is nonsexual as most of us human beings do. Although I sometimes again experience eroticized or sexual attractions, they have dramatically decreased. For me, the eroticized same-sex attractions usually surface when I feel shame, or I am comparing myself in a negative way to other men or am feeling insecure or when I am triggered from memories. When this happens, I see it as an indication of a need that should be met in healthy chaste ways. If I work through this and meet those needs, stop the negative self-talk or stop comparing myself to other men, then the sexual charge dissipates. For me, the sexual charge for same-sex attractions really began as nonsexual, starting at a very early age. These attractions for me were always about a longing to be accepted and connected to others.

I was looking at some older journals and found some beautiful examples of how through the Holy Spirit, I can get my needs met, causing the potential sexual charge to dissipate before it turns into something more. Here is a 2017 excerpt of just one of many times this happened:

Today, I had one of these moments of affirmation by a man, and it neutralized any potential sexual charges. Today at the gym, I did my workout and then chose to go to the sauna. I am somewhat new to the sauna and as a result a little fearful. Facing this fear is one of the reasons why I go in there, besides to relax and release toxins. In embracing my fears, I realize that the negative thoughts or worries that I don't fit in with other men aren't true. I have learned that I do fit in the world of men and am so grateful. Even so, sometimes I worry about what the conversation might be in that sauna. But I have learned that just because I am not into sports or objectifying women does not mean I don't belong. I used to think that this is what masculinity is and have learned that this is not true.

Jesus, in my opinion, is the model of pure masculinity and he indeed didn't objectify women. Although there is no record of him speaking about sports, (he might have), there are many examples of him living out pure masculinity. He was a leader, protector, and provider. He was determined, persevered in the most painful of circumstances, spoke in truth despite the consequences, reached out in love and of course, sacrificed his life freely, knowing that he was to endure much humiliation, pain, and suffering, but did so all out of true authentic love for us.

So, I am in there, and a younger man wearing nothing but a pair of shorts and extremely ripped with muscles and tattoos (which usually are a sexual charge for me and always have been) came in. The other guy left, and it was just he and I. He looked at my shirt which was an American Coaster Enthusiasts t-shirt with logo in the style of a Harley Davidson symbol. He then asked me about my bikes. When I told him that it wasn't a Harley shirt but a roller coaster shirt, he then spoke of how he also loves roller coasters. He wanted to know which coasters I liked, and we had a conversation. As we shared back and forth, I no longer noticed the muscles or the tattoos and instead saw his humanity as I took him off the pedestal. The sexual charge was neutralized before it was ignited. Back in high school, I was terrified to go to the locker room in fear I would be made fun of or told to leave because I didn't belong. Not facing that fear only intensified the fear, the shame and the misdirected sexualization of something that wasn't sexual to me in the first place. Today, at the gym, neutralizing experiences like this continue to happen which affirm me as a man by another man. This tells me that I do belong to the world of men.

Having conversations with men at the gym, while working out or in the locker room or now even in the sauna are ways in which I am affirmed as a man. It might not seem like it to the typical guy, but for me … it is.

Authentic Love

As I mentioned, I never recognized the masculinity I possessed when I was young and thought I was different from my other peers. I didn't look for the commonalities because my shame of this perceived difference was overwhelming. When I am affirmed by other men, as a man, my confidence grows and the need to possess what I think I lack dissipates. Since I sexualized this need that for me wasn't sexual in the first place, it only makes sense that when I am affirmed, the eroticized charge disappears.

I now have close male friendships in which I can be completely vulnerable and feel authentically accepted and loved as a friend and brother in Christ. This has been what I have longed for all my life. After all these years, I only recently began facing the emotional wounds that have scarred me from the sexual choices made throughout my life. I buried these wounds of shame deep inside, and, after all these years, it began to surface. I never realized how these choices have hurt me deeply. Although I didn't realize it, the promiscuous acting out seriously impacted how I viewed myself. Even though not all people have this shared experience, I know that I am far from alone. I recently finished counseling with a Christian therapist who helped me gain healing over the shame. She also helped me embrace the truth about who I really am as a child of God.

I am so grateful to God for His healing, His mercy, His truth, His love and for His hope. Earlier, I mentioned that I verbally forgave my father, but I have learned since then, that forgiveness is a process. My father passed away in 1996, and I was thankful that I was able to do this before he left this world. However, there were still many scars left in my heart from the abuse and anger, and I blamed him for much of my pain. God has brought me a long way on this journey upwards in forgiveness. I no longer think of my father and feel anger. I can honestly say I love my dad and mean this sincerely in my heart. This was a long slow process but was solidified in Christian counseling. I now understand that he did the best he could with his own inner turmoil. We all have crosses to carry. One of mine is same-sex attractions. He had his own which made it difficult for him to be a loving father. Through God, I now experience peace regarding my dad. I used to have a hard time relating to the Creator of the universe as my Heavenly Father, but now it's more comfortable and natural. As a result, I experience a more profound longing to grow and pursue holiness even more than I did before. In the past, if someone asked who I was, I would have said, I was a gay man.

Today, I know that is not my identity. There is so much more to who I am. Who am I? I am David. A Catholic man of God.

A message to those who experience same sex attractions and want to live chaste lives according to the Church teachings:

You are not alone. If you are Catholic, please check out Courage International at www.couragerc.org. Look to see if there is a chapter near you and if not, then get involved in a phone group or email group. God made us for relationship. We are not meant to live the Christian life alone. It is important to have authentic chaste friendships that support us. You do not have to do this alone. It is a wonderful feeling knowing I am not alone and that I have brothers and sisters who have my back, who pray for me and understand my journey. The Courage web site does much more than connect you to meetings. It is filled with resources, articles, books, talks and videos that can bring encouragement and insight in walking this journey. May God bless you and fill your life with His truth, authentic love and hope.

Acknowledgements

I want to thank my friend John Laney: John, thank you for your hard work in typesetting this booklet, for creating the beautiful cover, assisting in editing and more importantly for your encouragement, support and friendship.

I want to thank my friend Mary W: Thanks, Mary, for your tremendous help in the editing of this booklet as well as being a cheer leader, supporter and friend.

Thank you, Dr. John Bergsma. You have been strong supporter of my speaking on this topic and sharing my story. Thank you for your prayers and for believing in me and this work. It was your recognition of the importance of this project, that motivated me to self-publish this testimony of God's Truth, Love and Hope. Thank you for your support and for your heartfelt and beautiful foreword. I am humbled by your words. You are a man I have looked up to since I first heard you speak at a conference years ago, (before I pursued my MA at Franciscan) and, I am honored to know you. Thank you again for your time, encouragement and beautiful words.

I want to thank my friends Lisa Mladinich, Allison Ricciardi: Thank you for taking the time to read, and for writing beautiful endorsements. Thank you also for your suggestions, encouragement and support. God has blessed me by bringing both of you into my life.

Thank you, Dr. Patrick Lee, for being supportive back when I used to give talks at the University, and for continuing to do so, by taking the time to read and to write a great endorsement of the booklet. Thank you for your very kind words.

Notes

1 John-Andrew O'Rourke, dir., "The Third Way: Homosexuality and the Catholic Church," Blackstone Films, 2014.

2 Catechism of the Catholic Church, Second Edition. Paragraphs 2357-2358.

3 David Prosen, *Accompanying Those with Same-Sex Attractions: A Guide for Catholics.* Huntington, Indiana: Our Sunday Visitor, 2019.

Made in the USA
Monee, IL
06 September 2020